This book belongs to:

JB — Jessex B

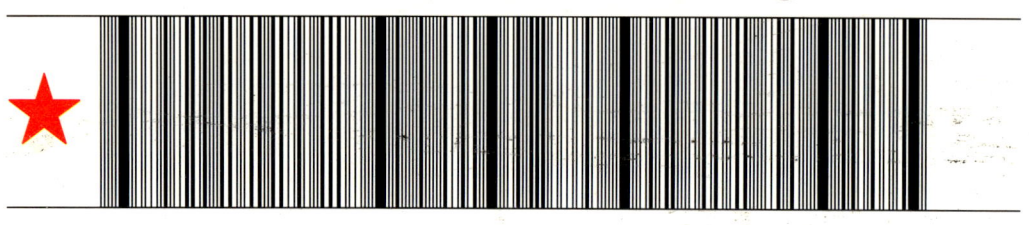

My First Animal Book

Written by Susan Smith
Illustrated by Larry Daste
Electronic Speech by Maurice Wong

Meet the animals

that live on the farm.

cow

chicken

horse

goat

turkey

bear

elk

owl

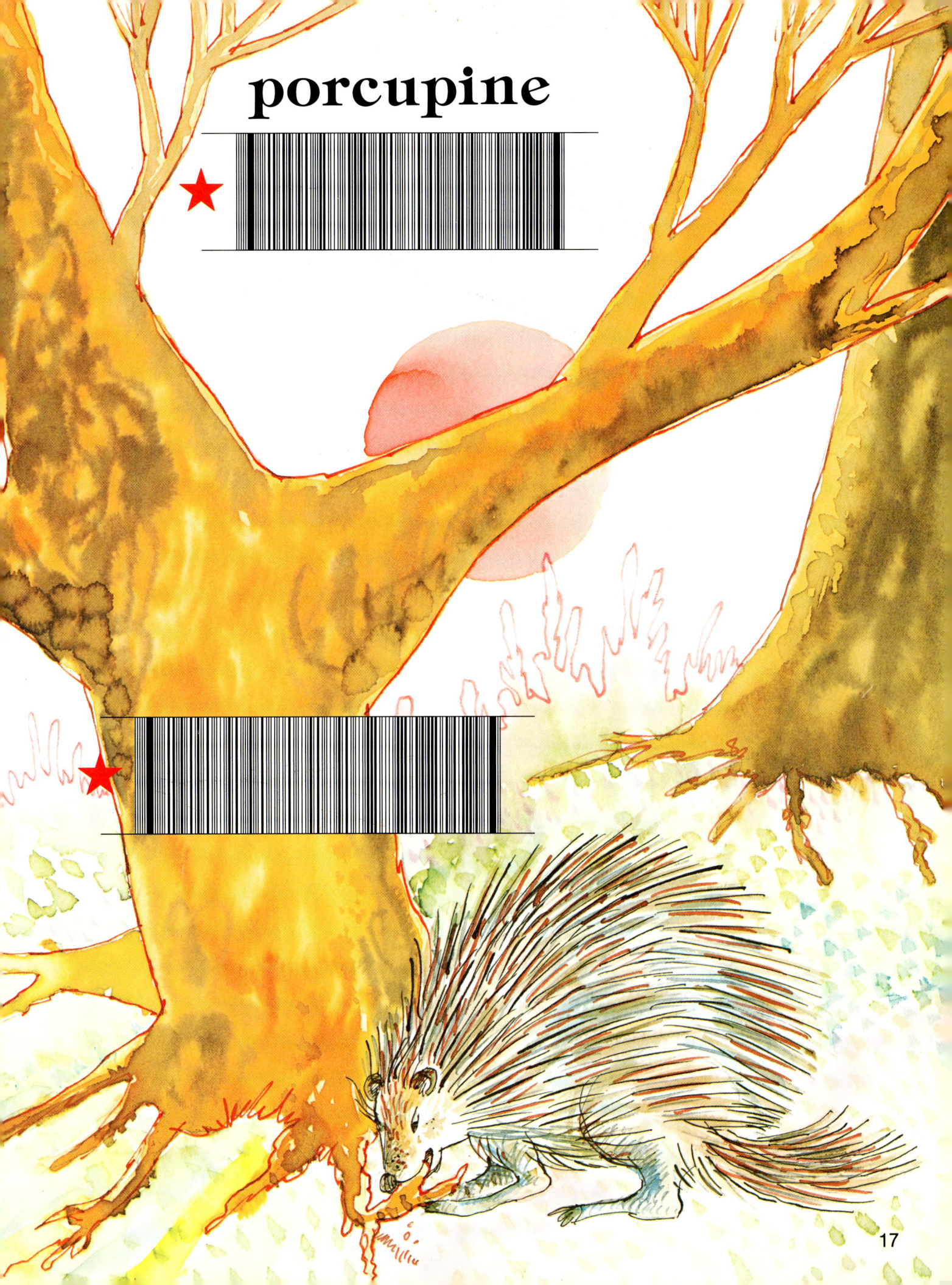
porcupine

rabbit

squirrel

Meet the animals

★

that live in the jungle.

★

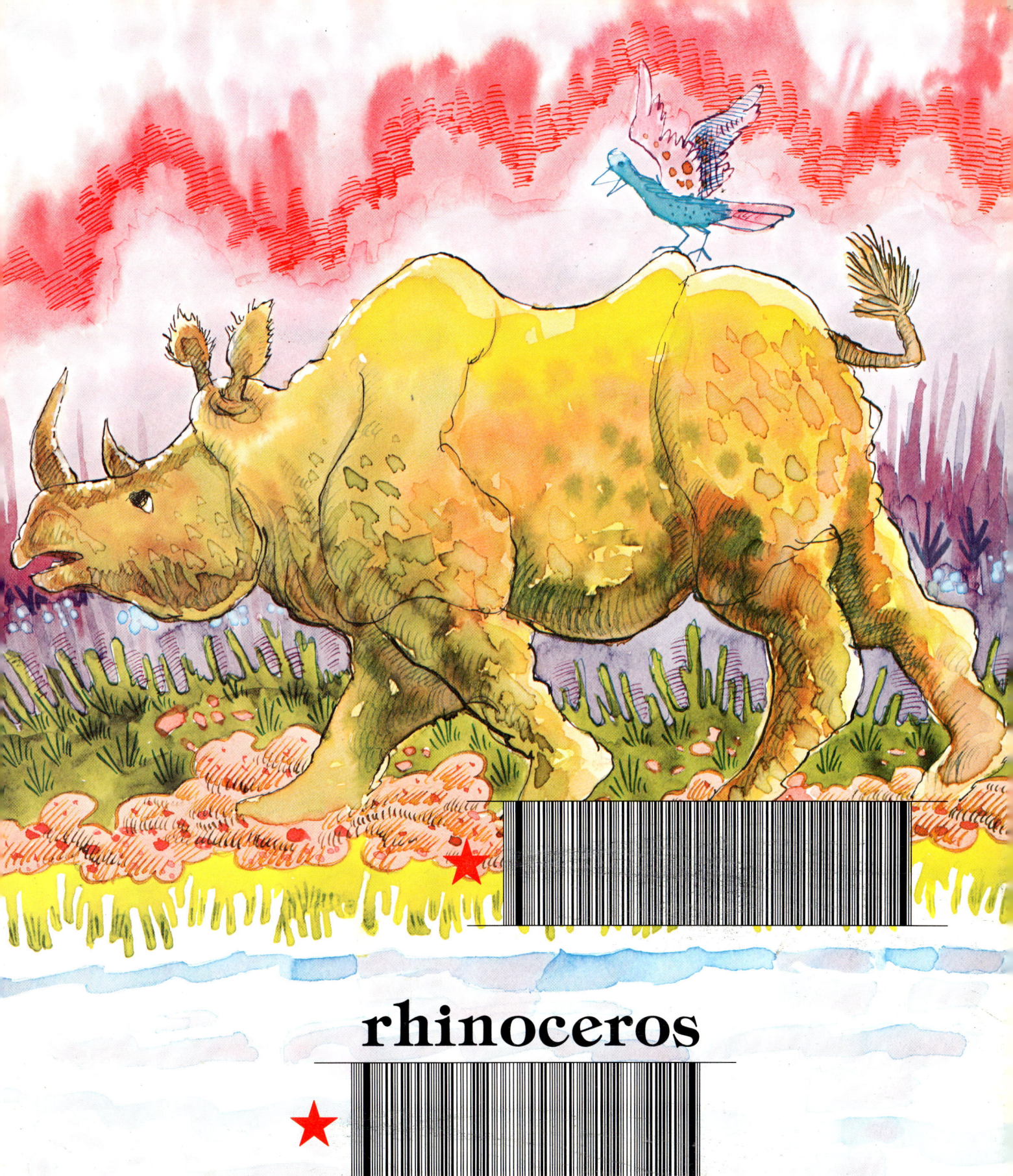

rhinoceros

elephant

chimpanzee

Meet the animals

that live in the sea.

crab

electric eel

sea horse

dolphin

octopus

Meet the animals

that live at home.

goldfish

canary

dog

at home.

on the farm.

Match sounds to animals!

Find an animal

whose name

begins with _____

bear

elephant

dog

How many hidden animals can you find?

DEAR PARENT:

For detailed information about the **Magic Wand Speak & Learn**™ system and the Speaking Reader Books, see the Parent's Letter enclosed with the **Magic Wand Speak & Learn** or write:

Texas Instruments Incorporated
Consumer Relations Department
P.O. Box 53
Lubbock, Texas 79408

If you have further questions, call Consumer Relations toll free at (800) 858-4565. Consumers outside the contiguous United States may call (806) 741-4800 (we regret that we cannot accept collect calls at this number).

LOOK FOR THESE TITLES FROM THE MAGIC WAND™ SPEAKING LIBRARY:

Level 1 — Toddler
Mister Rogers'® Planet Purple
My First Animal Book

Level 2 — Preschool
The Droopy Dragon
Talking E.T.™ Wordbook**
The Alphabet Zoo
The Noisy Number Robots
PicturePages® Makes Science Simple***
The Berenstain Bears'™ Olympics

Level 3 — Early Elementary
The Sprites' Adventures on Earth
The Wonderful Sound Store
The Amazing Spider-Man® in the Skyscraper Caper*
The Berenstain Bears™ on the Job
The Great Monster Party
Zany Zingers
Scooter Computer and Mr. Chips™****

*The Amazing Spider-Man and distinctive likeness thereof is a trademark of the Marvel Comics Group, a division of Cadence Industries Corporation, and is used with permission.

**E.T. and the E.T. character are a trademark of and licensed by Universal City Studios, Inc.

***PicturePages is a trademark of PicturePages, Inc.

****American Broadcasting Companies, Inc.

Texas Instruments invented the integrated circuit, the microprocessor and the microcomputer, which have made TI synonymous with reliability, affordability and compactness.